Dream High

Do you have a dream?

Sheena S.Lee

This book is for all those who have a dream. Don't give on that dream and achieve it.

Table of Contents:

Title page:	1
Dedication page:	3
Chapter 1:	5
Chapter 2:	9
Chapter 3:	12
Chapter 4:	14
Chapter 5:	16
Chapter 6:	18
Chapter 7:	20
Chapter 8:	22
Chapter 9:	24
Chapter 10:	28
Authors bio:	29

Chapter 1: Hae Boong

Summer is almost over, and I have to convince my dad to let me go to the best arts school. He thinks I should go to Korea's top elite school, but I want to go to Kirin Arts School. Kirin Arts School, a school were you can focus on singing, dancing, acting, and even composing. I always loved performing arts, and this school is perfect for me. This morning's conversation was so complicated.

"Have you thought of which high school you want to go to?" said Dad.

"Yes, I want to go to Kirin Arts School," I said.

"I want you to go to a top Elite school," said Dad. "When you go to that stupid arts school, how is that going to make my business look?"

"Ugh, your business is always first for you, and that's all you care about. Ever since mom died, you never cared about Hae Ri or me; only your precious JO Group," she snapped.

"Make breakfast for you and your sister; I have to get to work," he said coldly. "We will talk when I come back home."

"Whatever. Hyun Mi and Min Kkuk are coming over," said Hae Boong. "Are you coming home for dinner. "Starting to cross her hands, and giving her father attitude.

"No, I have a company dinner tonight, so eat by yourselves," said Dad. He left for work muttering "teenagers."

How can he be so selfish? thought Hae Boong.

"Unni, Unni, Unni," called Hae Ri "when is Hyun Mi and Min Kkuk coming?"

"They're coming in a few minutes. Why do you call the by their name?" said Hae Boong. "Like you call me Unni, you have to call your older sister Unni. So call

Hyun Mi unni. You also have to call Min Kkuk, oppa, because it means older brother," lectured Hae Boong.

"Okay," Hae Ri said sadly.

A few minutes passed and the girls heard a knock on the door.

"They must be here," exclaimed Hae Ri!

"Hey," said Hyun Mi.

"What's up?" said Min Kkuk.

"Oppa, lets go to the park," said Hae Ri.

"No, we will go later," said Hae Boong. "Eat your breakfast and change to your clothes."

So the three friends were now in Hae Boong's room while they talked about how they had to convince their parents to let them go to Kirin Arts School. The three always had many common reasons why they were friends but the main reason, was because they all had the same dream. That dream was to become an idol. They all wanted to do what they love, either if it was singing, dancing, or acting. They all had their own reasons why they loved to dance or sing or even act, and that was how they formed their dreams.

"So, how are you guys going to go to school now?" said Min Kkuk. "My mom said yes, but we have to worry about the tuition."

Oh, I almost forgot that Kkuk Yi might not have the money for the tuition because it is still pricey. I wonder how his family . . . as Hae Boong's thought were disrupted by Hyun Min talking.

"Well, my dad said yes last night, and he applied both Kkuk Yi and me up for the school," said Hyun Mi.

"He did what," said Min Kkuk in shock.

"Well, he knows you and your family, and he sent your mom a text saying he will," complained Hyun Mi. "I thought she told you because your mom said okay."

"Well, thank you," replied Kkuk Yi "but this is the last time I'm taking big money like that from you."

The three friends talked and laughed all day and even took Hae Ri to the park. They went to the practice room at their old school, and they practiced for their Kirin freshman auditions. They had a lot to worry about because they heard that the auditions were very tough. It didn't matter if they had talent or not, because it was if you were able to try hard. There were people from all over Korea trying to get into this school, and they had training from classes that the three never had. It wasn't only them who had the dream to become the best idol.

After practicing, they went back home, and found Hae Ri watching TV in the living room. Hyun Mi and Min Kkuk got all their stuff and left to go to their homes. The two sisters made their dinner together and waited for their dad to come home. The girls watched their own dramas on their own. A few hours passed, and their dad came back home wanting to talk to Boong Yi.

"I've thought about it and you can go to your school," he said, "but you have to make sure you don't cause any trouble."

Hae Boong Yi was silent from shock that her father finally said yes. "Thank you, thank you, thank you!" she said. With excitement she hugged her dad and he kissed her, saying to be good at the new school.

"And if you cause any trouble, I will have Secretary Kim transfer you to an elite school, so be good."

"But, but," whined Boong Yi, "fine, I guess that's fair. Thank you so much."

Boong Yi was so excited that she went straight into her room and called her friends and told them about her father's approval. They agreed to meet the next day to practice for their auditions. She was so excited she couldn't sleep, and all she could dream about was her becoming the best idol ever. The chance was right in front of her and she would do anything, everything to make her father proud.

Chapter 2:Hyun Mi

"I'm home," Hyun Mi said as she walked through her doors. The first person to meet her was not even human, but her cute Shih Tzu, Bennett. "Hi Bennett."

"How was your day?" said Hyun Mi's mom. "Mi Na, dinner's ready, so call your father "

"Okay" Hyun Mi said as she walked to he father's study. "Dad time to eat" she told him.

"So, Mi Na, how was your day?" her dad asked.

"It was fine," she replied. After dinner, Hyun Mi did the dishes and went to her room. She had a lot to think of like what she would wear to the audition, what to sing, and what to dance.

Mi Na got a call from Boong Yi on the way home, so that means all of the three friends were going to Kirin Arts school. Mi Na remembered when she first met Boong

Yi at their Dad's company. Their dads were the co-CEOs of JO Group and that was when Boong Yi and Mi Na became friends. They did everything together since they were 6-years-old. Then in first grade they met Min Kkuk where he was new to the school. Ever since then the three were like The Three Musketeers. They always liked to dance and sing together at their school's practice room.

The next morning, the three rendezvous at their school to practice for their audition. The three decided to do trio auditions, to sing and dance together. They chose a piece that expresses all three of them. They practiced hard and were able to master it together because in a few days, they were going to go to the auditions.

"So, when do you want to practice again?" asked Kkuk Yi.

Mi Na replied, "Tomorrow, because the auditions are the day after tomorrow."

"Alright, then I have to go. Hae Ri is home by herself," said Boong Yi.

"Bye," Min Kkuk and Mi Na said at the same time.

The two went to Min Kkuk's family restaurant, where Min Kkuk's little sister Min Ji and his mom was there.

"Hi, Mrs. Lee," I said

"Oh, hi Mi Na," said Mrs. Lee. "Do you want some food, you must be hungry because of practice."

"Yes, please," I replied.

As they waited for their food, Min Kkuk was playing with his sister, and they took her out to get some food ingredients. While they were at the store, Min Ji wanted a toy but her brother didn't have the money, so Mi Na payed for it.

"Oppa, can you buy me this toy?" Min Ji asked?

"Next time," he replied.

"Do you want me to buy it for you?" asked Hyun Mi as she grabbed the toy and walked to the cashier.

"Yay!" exclaimed Min Ji.

"Say thank you," scolded Kkuk Yi.

"Thank you, Unni," said Min Ji with a big smile. "Let's go back home. Mommy is waiting."

"Oh, yeah, let's go," I said.

When we went back to the restaurant Mrs. Lee was waiting for us with a nice home cooked meal. After I ate, Kkuk Yi and I walked back to my place.

The three met again at their school and practiced one more time. They all went home early because the auditions were tomorrow. They were all nervous, but went home early and woke up the next day feeling fresh.

Chapter 3: Min Kkuk

The D-Day has finally come. The auditions were here. Kkuk Yi needed to get in this school more than anyone, because if he became an idol then he can support his family. He wanted to get big, so he can quit his part-time jobs. Min Kkuk was very nervous as he met his friends. They all took the bus to the school and arrived on time. Everyone was all practicing their singing and dancing. The school was filled with freshmen; it was unbelievable. So the three thought that it was best to start practicing.

"One, two, three, four," counted Hae Boong "one, and two, and three."

By this time, all eyes were at us. Everyone stopped what they were doing and stared at us. It was as if everyone was interested at us, and the juniors walked toward us.

"It looks like we got a little freshmen trio who thinks they're that great," said a tall girl in front of a bunch of girls.

"Ri Ah, lets leave them alone. What use would it do if we get in trouble?" said another girl who was next to the girl named Ri Ah.

"Joo Ah, did you forget that all the teachers are too busy right now?" said Ri Ah.

"Well, these three aren't going to get in that easily, if they practice here like this," said another girl.

"What do you mean?" Kkuk Yi asked, as he was starting to get a little angry at these juniors.

"Ha Nyul, don't freak them out too much," said Joo Ah.

"Well they should know that our school doesn't take more than 150 freshmen," said Ha Nyul.

"What!" exclaimed Hae Boong.

"What makes you think that we won't get into this school?" asked Hyun Mi. "You never seen us do anything."

Then the announcements called the three friends for their auditions.

"Student number 1256 Kim Hae Boong, student number 1257 Choi Hyun Mi, and student number 1258 Lee Min Kkuk, please come to the audition room for your auditions," announced the PA system. "I repeat student number 1256 Kim Hae Boong, student number 1257 Choi Hyun Mi, and student number 1258 Lee Min Kkuk, please come to the audition room for your auditions."

"Well, it seems like you are going to see how we get into this school soon," I said. Kkuk Yi hated girls like this who judged them and didn't even know them.

"Well we are watching, so show us what you got," Ri Ah said.

Chapter 4: Ul Bong

The three friends walked into the audition room and the audition was monitored so everyone can watch. Everyone was anticipating for this auditions because the juniors challenged them. Even Ul Bong was interested and he was in his grandfather's office until he heard all the fuss outside.

Ul Bong is a privileged child from wealth by his grandfather, but he grew up in his father's hometown, which was in the country side of Korea. He has a accent from the countryside and is coming back to Seoul to attend his grandfather's school. Ul Bong is a great dancer that has a strong potential for it. He went downstairs and saw the audition from the monitor with the juniors, who despise the three.

Inside the audition room the three were getting ready to sing and dance to their song called Dream High.

The song starts and everyone at the school were on their tippy toes. Then they started.

"Dream high," Kkuk Yi said as the music started.

"I dream high, I can dream a dream," as Hyun Mi began the song. Then as all three started dancing the judges were all interested.

Ri Ah in the other room was shocked on how good they were. When it was her audition she barely passed the judges. She got into this school because a teacher felt pity for her. The first day of her school a senior gave her the K pendent and it gave her more confidence. She was a better performer because of that necklace.

Now, the song was finished. The three felt confident because they didn't make any mistakes and gave the judges their best performance. It was time for the judges to tell them how they did and if they passed.

"I say that all three students pass," said the first judge.

"I agree also," said the second judge who was next to the first judge. "I really like your performance," as she hummed their song.

Now all the judges looked at the principal. "I am so pleased with your audition. The judges agreed to have all three pass. Welcome to Kirin Arts School, because as of this moment you three are freshman of this school. Oh, and thank you for the best performance we have seen so far," said the principal.

The three were jumping up and down. They all passed the auditions.

"THANK YOU SO MUCH!" Hyun Mi and Hae Boong exclaimed to the judges.

Chapter 5: Hae Boong

After they left the audition room, they met the three juniors again. They were walking towards them and everyone in the school was all around the six students.

"Do you have anything to say?" asked Hae Boong.

"Do you have anything to say?" mocked Ha Nyul.

"Well, congratulations," Ri Ah said with a sarcastic tone in her voice. "Oh, and here have this," as she gave her a bronze pendant with a chain on it.

"What's this," Hae Boong said as she received the pendant.

"It's more or less of a tradition to pass this done to freshman," said Ri Ah "This was K's pendant and he passed it down to seniors who passed it down to freshman then to us. Now it's your turn, I think you will need this more than we will."

"I will see you when school starts then." Hyun Mi said. As she started to walk she stopped in front of a monitor. The monitor showed the audition room and it was Ul Bong's turn for the auditions.

"What, why did you stop walking?" asked Kkuk Yi.

"He is really good at dancing!" said Hyun Mi.

They watched his auditions and left. The day was tough but the four students got into the school that they will be attending for their high school years.

It's the first day of school and Hae Boong was almost late. She woke up a little late and missed her bus. She called a taxi and was able to make it to school on time.

"That will be $12," said the taxi driver asking for the payment of the ride.

"Here you go," said Boong Yi as she gave the driver the money.

"Thank you" he said.

Then he drove away and Boong Yi walked toward the school. Mi Na and Min Kkuk were waiting for her at the front of the school but there was someone else. It was the boy who she watched dancing at the monitor at the auditions. He was teaching Kkuk Yi the moves he did for the auditions.

"Hey guys, let's go in," suggested Kkuk Yi.

"Hi, I'm Ul Bong," he said Boong Yi while they were walking.

"Hi," Hae Boong said back to Ul Bong.

They went in to find the school filled with student getting their uniforms and class schedules. They got in line and got their uniforms, when they were told surprising news about their schedules.

Chapter 6: Hyun Mi

The four were really shocked with the news they got from the teacher.

"Oh, hi, I'm Teacher Kang of dancing. So how do we have here" she introduced her to us.

"Well we are, Kim Hae Boong, Choi Hyun Mi, Lee Min Kkuk, and Jung Ul Bong" said Kkuk Yi.

"Right," as she got her phone and called someone. "Mr. Lee the four students are here."

"Are they together," he asked.

"Yes, they are all here together."

"Good, send them up."

"Yes, sir" she replied, "the four of you go into the principal office."

The four exchanged nervous glances and walked up to the office; as they walked through the office they met all their teachers. They all looked at each other and went into the office.

"Come in," said Mr. Lee.

"Hello," they all said but Ul Bong who just walked to the couch.

"Come and sit down," he said with a smile.

"Hi, Grandpa," Ul Bong said.

"GRANDPA!" they three exclaimed.

"Alright let's get into business," Ul Bong's grandpa said.

He told the four of them with their skills and grade levels they will be studying with the s juniors who are getting ready to debut. They were going to be attending a different schedule than the regular freshmen.

"But their were so many people with skills why us," Mi Na asked.

"The teachers and I like your friendship and we will like to create a group with the three of you and Ul Bong together if you like this request."

"That sounds good," Boong Yi said.

"Well that is enough chit chat, here are your schedules now go to class," he said as he was sending them away.

Chapter 7: Min Kkuk

They all had the same classes and their first class was dancing with Teacher Kang. They walked into the dance room and found trouble. They found the juniors who were in their class. Then they saw Ri Ah, Joo Ah, and Ha Nyul.

"Why are you guys here," said Ri Ah who was as shocked as like all of them. "This is a private class for students who are getting ready to debut. Not for little freshmen who don't know the basics."

"That's why they are here," said Teacher Kang. "They are here to learn, so they will also be able to debut."

"But that's not fair," complained Ha Nyul.

"If that's not fair, then the door is wide open so you can leave," snapped Ms. Kang. "Do you think the world is fair. If you can't deal with this competition then you shouldn't be in this field of entertainment. If you look at them like they are a threat then you are hopeless."

"Whatever," Ha Nyul said while rolling her eyes.

The seven of the students went for tough training, for the next four months, and still they hated each other. At the end of the new semester there is a showcase where their will be a chance to sign a contract with entertainment labels that will help the debut. The three juniors are getting ready do debut as a trio for the showcase. The four new friends were now really close and wear getting ready to debut together. It was time for them to debut but only one group will debut and now one knows who it will be.

"Alright the show case is coming up," Ms. Kang said as she came into the dance room. "What song will you guys be doing?"

"The three of is will be doing the song Superstar by Hershe," said Ri Ah. She turned to look at us with a face expression that read *beat that.*

"Good choice," Teacher Kang said "Now, how about you guys what song will you guys be doing?"

"We will be doing Dream High, like their auditions!" said Ul Bong.

"Okay, but this will be a little difficult because that was for a trio, you guys are now a group of four," said Teacher Kang   The seven of the students were starting to practice from lyrics to dance steps. They all were getting ready and were not paying attention to the other team. They couldn't afford to make a mistake like last time.

Chapter 8: Ul Bong

It was the opening act for the new students were the three juniors were supposed to set a stage to debut. There were reporters, agency represents, and other school reps. The three juniors were getting ready for their part of the stage were agencies can recruit them. Right before the stage Ri Ah and her friends came to see the four friends who were watching. She told them to watch and learn. For Ri Ah, it was a big day because her father was coming to watch her. She was also really nervous because her father did not approve of Ri Ah wanting to be a singer and it was her first time performing without he pendant. It was time, and the three Ri Ah, Joo Ah, and Ha Nyul was on the stage and in their positions.

Joo Ah began to sing "I know you will be a superstar."

They were doing well, when all of a sudden, Ri Ah lost focus. It seems that she got eye contact with her father. She got all the dance moves wrong and fell not he end. From this distraction she was not able to debut and let her friends down. Her father was so disappointed he left, and Ri Ah was so depressed. She couldn't lift her head up for a long time, then she got a second chance. They were practicing, and all the teachers came in to talk, about the showcase.

"Alright, it's time to make the finishing touches for the showcase," said Kang Teacher.

"Yes, you all will be competing against each other, the groups, to debut," Mr. Lee said. "All of you will be able debut but the choice of the lane is up to you. It will be on how you impress the agencies. If you do well you can get a contract that will take care of your career."

"Now, if you mess up get up and keep going on with the song," Ms. Kang said facing Ri Ah.

"Alright, that's all now, keep working," said Mr. Lee.

The four went to Kkuk Yi's restaurant for lunch. They all went in and found Min Ji in the restaurant playing with the toy Mi Na bought her. She was so happy to see them again especially her brother. In a few weeks they were going to preform, so they had to be very cautious. They all went out for a walk in the park; then there was a car that was coming fast at Min Ji. Kkuk Yi took her sister out of the way and took the hit for her.

Chapter 9: Hae Boong

They were at a hospital now with Kkuk Yi in surgery. Ms. Lee closed down the restaurant and met the kids at the hospital. Min Ji was in a stake of shock and couldn't stop crying. She was in her mother's arms and blaming herself it was her fault.

"Mommy, what do I do? Oppa got hurt because of me," Min Ji said as she was crying.

"It's okay your brother will be fine" her mother replied.

The rest of the friends were worried about Kkuk Yi. The teachers came to meet them at the hospital to see if he was ok. Then the doctor came out of the surgery room.

Ms. Lee went up to the doctor and asked if her son was okay. "Doctor the surgery was successful, right? Please tell me that my son is safe," she pleaded.

"Don't worry, ma'am, the surgery was very successful. Can I have a guardian to talk to please," said the doctor.

"Ms. Lee, I will go to talk to the doctor, you should wait for Min Kkuk to come out," offered Ms. Kang.

"Thank You," said Ms. Lee.

Hae Boong went with Ms. Kang to the doctor's office. The doctor said that the leg was fine it was just that he had to rest the leg for a few days.

"Thank, the Lord he is all right," exclaimed Boong Yi. Then she filled out the paperwork and went to Kkuk Yi's hospital bed. She found him awake and in his arms his sister. She was tired from crying, and now was sleeping in her brother's warm arms.

"Are you felling any better?" asked Mi Na.

"Yah, I will be fine," said Kkuk Yi. "Well you guys have to get back to school now you guys have practice, remember."

Boong Yi, Mi Na, and Ul Bong went back to school with Ms. Kang. Then they met the juniors waiting for them. For the first time they were being really nice about the situation.

"Is Kkuk Yi okay?" asked Joo Ah.

"Yah, he is good thanks for asking," Hae Boong replied.

"Well, we have English Class with Mr. Yang today, lets go to class," said Ha Nyul.

"Alright let's go," said Ul Bong.

For the next few days it was all the same. Take classes, visit Kkuk Yi, and practice more. Finally, Kkuk Yi was discharged from the hospital and came back to school. He was perfectly fine just had to practice a little more.

The first few times he forgot the dance moves but then he got back up. From time to time Kkuk Yi's leg hurt, but after some painkillers he was better. The performance was tomorrow and all the students were nervous for the performance. They were dismissed early, so for good luck they gathered in a huddle and put their hands in and screamed "good luck." They went to their dorms and rested for the rest of the day.

    Hae Boong was so excited her dad and her sister was going to watch her. The next day she woke up early and got dressed and headed for the school with Mi Na. The rest of the school, was cleaning the school and getting chairs ready for the guests. They went to the dance room and found the rest of the friends there,getting ready and in the clothes. They were all practicing their parts and their dance moves. It wasn't only the seven, for the showcase there were other people going solo or in a group like them. Now, it was show time.

The first performance was the juniors who went with the name of Complex Trio saying they are different in many ways. This time Ri Ah didn't freeze up and they all did very well. Then it was their turn and they came up with the name of Dreamers. They called themselves Dreamers because they were all kids who had a dream to be who they are now. When the whole performance was finished they all gathered up on stage and so did the agencies. One bye one they were all chosen.

"Now, JYP Entertainment will chose The Dreamers," announced Ms. Kang. "And S.M Entertainment will take Complex Trio under their label."

They were jumping up and down because they became busy with their schedules. Now they were big

Hallu stars and were going on tour for 200 days. Back just in time for graduation.

It was graduation day and they all came back at the same time. Ri Ah, Joo Ah, Ha Nyul, Ul Bong, Kkuk Yi, Hyun Mi, and Boong Yi all arrived at Kirin Arts School at the same time to see reporters waiting for their arrival. They were all friends now and had to go in for graduation day. They four was able to skip a few grade because of their rushed debut.

Mr. Lee and Ms. Kang together, gave out the diplomas and proudly announced the graduates of 2013. "Through the hardships and friendships you've made at this school, I proudly announce you graduates of Kirin Art School year 2013. You have all graduated, congratulations.

Chapter 10: Epilogue (8 years later)

Eight years later and they are all still doing pretty well. Ri Ah is a teacher at Kirin Arts School and Ha Nyul and Joo Ah owns a preschool together. Hae Boong is a learning business for her father's sake but is still a wonderful singing tutor. Hyun Mi became Korea's best actress and Ul Bong and Min Kkuk are called Dancing Duos, who are worldwide Hallyu stars. Min Ji and Hae Ri were attending Kirin Arts school and everyone was going to meet back at the school. For a showcase that Min Ji and Hae Ri were going to participate in and Ri Ah was their teacher.

They all met in front of the school and couldn't be happier to see each other. For the showcase, the girls did something that the seven could never think of. They invited the seven up onto the stage and made them sing.

In the end, they were all singing and dancing to their song Dream High. They were all happy together and nothing can make them felling better. This was the results of kids who had dreams, they were all happy in the end no matter the obstacles they faced. Do you have a dream?

Sheena Lee is a student at Notre Dame Academy. Her teacher told her that she had to write a novel for the  NaNoWriMo. She didn't know what to write and was wondering what she should write then it was time. Time to turn in the topic. She loves watching Korean drama and she came a cross the drama Dream High. She loved this drama and she watched the second season. She based her book on the third season getting her ideas from these dramas. Sheena made her book to be the third season for dream high. She wants everyone to have a dream.

www.ingramcontent.com/pod-product-compliance
Lightning Source LLC
LaVergne TN
LVHW050905220225
804315LV00007BA/518